COVENTRY
AT WAR

COVENTRY
AT WAR

DAVID MCGRORY

The
History
Press

I dedicate this book to those who lived, worked and died in Coventry during the war years.

First published in 1997
This edition published 2009

The History Press
The Mill, Brimscombe Port
Stroud, Gloucestershire, GL5 2QG
www.thehistorypress.co.uk

British Library Cataloguing in Publication Data.
A catalogue record for this book is available from the British Library.

ISBN: 978 0 7524 5328 6

Typesetting and origination by The History Press
Printed in Great Britain

CONTENTS

INTRODUCTION

In the summer of 1861 James Starley arrived in Coventry. The weaving industry had just collapsed and unemployed weavers could be seen standing in groups on street corners in the summer sun. Coventry was in industrial decline and many left the city, including 4,000 who emigrated.

Starley, with the help of Josiah Turner and a group of London investors, set up the Coventry Sewing Machine Company producing Starley's 'improved' sewing machine. Starley's mind later turned to the cycle, which had just taken off in France, and he decided to improve the machine and produce it in Coventry.

On his death Starley was hailed as the saviour of Coventry, for his introduction of cycle manufacturing to the city had led to massive industrial growth, making Coventry the greatest producer of cycles in the world.

As time passed the city and its population grew; many cycle manufacturers turned naturally to the production of the motor car and even light aircraft. The mechanical skills of Coventrians, old and new, were easily adaptable for such industrial metamorphosis. The seeds of mechanical industrialisation which Starley had sown would, unbeknown to him, have dire consequences in the following century as the Second World War cast its grim cloud across the land.

Before the outbreak of war, as in the First World War, Coventry's industries went into overdrive for war production. Armstrong Whitworth began making Whitley bombers; Humber produced troop transporters, scout and staff cars; Dunlop made wheel discs and brakes for fighters and bombers, and gun mechanisms for fighters such as the Spitfire. Even the traditional silk weaving industry, led by Cash's, supplied the air force with parachute gear.

To help protect war production shadow factories were set up around the city outskirts . . . war production was on full footing.

Men and women were needed to keep this production flowing and it was noted in 1941 that most worked twelve hour shifts. The city's population since 1931 had increased by 90,000, and in the first six months of the war a further 20,000 were added to the population, with another 36,000 expected.

The building of houses had stopped on the outbreak of war and all available houses were snapped up within hours of being vacated. In early 1941 25,000 people were recorded as being in lodgings, sometimes three men sharing a double bed. The Corporation eased the problem by opening hostels around the city in areas such as Keresley and Willenhall, hiring basic small rooms and cafeteria facilities. Food costs were kept down and many Government-run restaurants were opened; there was a huge increase in those who ate out. Many of course could afford to, as the average worker in Coventry earned around £10 a week before overtime. Coventry had become the El Dorado of the working classes, with car ownership becoming the highest in the land, until, of course, petrol rationing put an end to it.

Coventry's war industry inevitably made it a target for the Luftwaffe, whose first visit took place on 25 June 1940 when five bombs were dropped on Ansty Aerodrome. This was quickly followed by bombs in Hillfields, which resulted in sixteen fatalities. Coventry endured 41 actual raids and 373 siren alerts, the last being in August 1942. Two particularly ferocious raids took place on 8 and 10 April 1941.

The most notorious, of course, was that of 14–15 November 1940, which lasted for eleven long hours, making it the most concentrated bombing ever on an English city. After the destruction of Coventry's heart the Germans created a new word for destruction: 'Coventrated'. Many rumours surround this raid, such as that Churchill knew it was going to happen and sacrificed the city. These rumours, which appeared initially in one source, have been spread by others. They are untrue and this has been proved. It is a fact that on the afternoon of 14 November Churchill was being driven to Ditchley House, when he opened his yellow ULTRA dispatch box. On reading the contents of one paper he ordered his driver to return to Number 10, as he believed London was to be the target that night. On his arrival Churchill ordered his staff into the bunker, informing them that their young lives were important for the country's future. He himself, as was his custom when London was under threat, went on to the roof of the Air Ministry accompanied by General Ismay to await the bombers. The bombers never came and Churchill soon discovered their destination. Later, it is recorded he spent his time on the phone to Coventry's War Operation Centre under the post office, and also lost his cool with the officer in charge of air defence based on the Radford Road.

Other rumours abounded and still do to this day; bodies buried in air raid shelters, planes leaving question marks in the sky; even an IRA man sending a signal to German bombers from the tower of St Michael. This one was repeated to me recently as a fact. The truth behind this 'fact', however, is that it is pure fantasy originating from a fictional thriller called *The Coventry Option*, published in 1979. So much for facts.

The war period was an extraordinary period for all who lived through it. A period where all human emotions were stretched to the limits. A period which led to the most devastating events in Coventry's long and illustrious past. The war may be long gone, but the memories remain, and we all still live with the consequences of those dreadful nights, when the city was bombed into oblivion and memory. On that summer's day in 1861 what if . . . !

GREY CLOUDS
LOOMING, 1939

The hustle and bustle of Broadgate is brought to an abrupt halt on 25 August 1939. Five lay dead and dozens injured by an IRA bomb, which was left in the basket of a cycle between Burton's and Astley's. This was but a taste of what the future held for Coventry.

Looking up Broadgate from Owen's, early 1939. Little did the people of Coventry know what the near future held for their beloved city – a city that one pre-war novelist stated was one of the best preserved medieval cities in Europe.

Trams at Priestley's Bridge Depot, 1939. The two open-top trams could date back to as early as 1912, when Coventry Corporation purchased the Coventry Electric Tramways Company for £202,132. The trams on the right have had white lines painted under their lamps in preparation for the black-out. They would soon have lamp covers and subdued internal lighting.

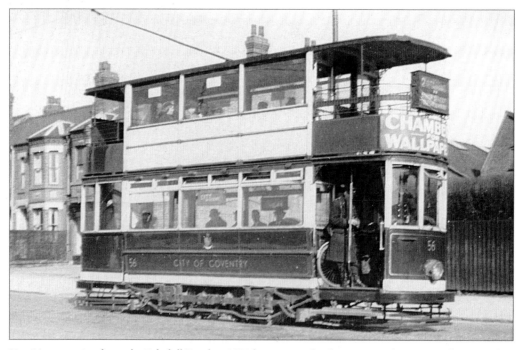

No. 56 tram going down the Foleshill Road in 1939 bearing much white paintwork owing to the impending black-out. Note the bicycle in the driver's section.

The no. 68 tram trundles past Edgewick Recreation Ground on the Foleshill Road at the beginning of 1939. By the park entrance is a poster calling for volunteers for the ARP services. Within the park was a trench shelter capable of holding 771 people.

The Duke of Kent visiting the Armstrong Whitworth Aircraft factory at Baginton, 1939. In the hangar stands an Ensign (right) and a Whitley bomber (back left).

A busy Broadgate photographed from the steps of the National Bank (now the National Westminster Bank) at the top of Broadgate, early 1939. Just over a year later this view would change forever.

Pre-war Hertford Street; most of the buildings up to the Pearl Assurance sign still stand. Beyond the sign is now the covered shopping area up to the post office. This mid-section was hit in November 1940 and April 1941.

The west end of the old cathedral photographed by Cliff Barlow of Holbrooks less than a year before its destruction. On the left is the tower arch and on the right the west door; between stands a wooden statue of St Michael carved, painted and gilded by Chipping Campden artist, Alex Miller. On 14 November the fire which destroyed the building first took hold in the far aisle on the right.

The beautiful interior of St Michael's photographed in 1935. The cathedral, a parish church until 1918, was considered by Sir Christopher Wren to be an architectural masterpiece. The cathedral enshrined 700 years of Coventry's past, a past which was destroyed by a few small incendiaries, no more than 15 in long.

Broadgate, looking down Hertford Street, 1939. Trams and buses cut through a busy rush hour. Both trams, nos 58 and 69, were purchased in 1931 and ran until 1940 to Bell Green and Stoke. The Keresley bus ran to the Shepherd and Shepherdess every fifteen minutes. The headline on the news-stand (far right), 'Lords Rush Through IRA Bill', refers to the recent IRA bomb outrages. Soon 'War' would be the headline.

An excellent view of Smithford Street taken from the second storey of the City Arcade, next to Woolworth's, on a busy Saturday in 1939. Note the sign by British Home Stores informing all that there is an air-raid shelter here capable of holding up to 330 people. Apart from Anderson shelters, other larger shelters had to be built throughout the city. By 14 November 1940 the National Emergency Committee had created enough trench, basement and street shelters to accommodate 170,344 citizens. The *Midland Daily Telegraph* reported on 29 September 1938, a year before the outbreak of war, that up to 600 workmen had begun work on air-raid shelters in parks and recreation grounds. These were Spencer Park, Memorial Park (near Kenilworth Road), Styvechale Common (Coat of Arms/Green Lane corner), Primrose Hill Park (high ground), Radford Recreation Ground (high ground near Jaguar-Daimler), Moseley Avenue (near school and library), Nauls Mill Park (near Middleborough Road entrance), Radford Common (parallel to Holland Road), Edgewick Recreation Ground (near school), Hearsall Common (parallel to Earlsdon Avenue), Whitley Common (junction London/Daventry Roads), Binley Road (near Bulls Head), Barras Heath (children's playground), Longford Recreation Ground (high ground), Gosford Green (playing area), Livingstone Road (opposite Baths), Cheylesmore Estate (by pool), Bird Street (old bowling green), Holbrook Lane (end of Jackson Road), Foleshill Park (at front), Greyfriars Green (Queen's Road end) and finally Corporation Street (between Fleet/Fretton Streets). These shelters and more would soon be filled to capacity; some people went down them once, but never again – as generally they were cramped, smelly and damp. Many died when shelters took direct hits but the majority survived and the shelters proved their worth, saving many thousands of lives.

The eleventh hour of the eleventh day of the eleventh month; this is the last spontaneous 'silence' before Coventry was blitzed. All stand still, hats removed, heads bowed, as the clock in Broadgate approaches the eleventh hour and the bell of St Michael's strikes. No more 'silences' would be held till after the war ended.

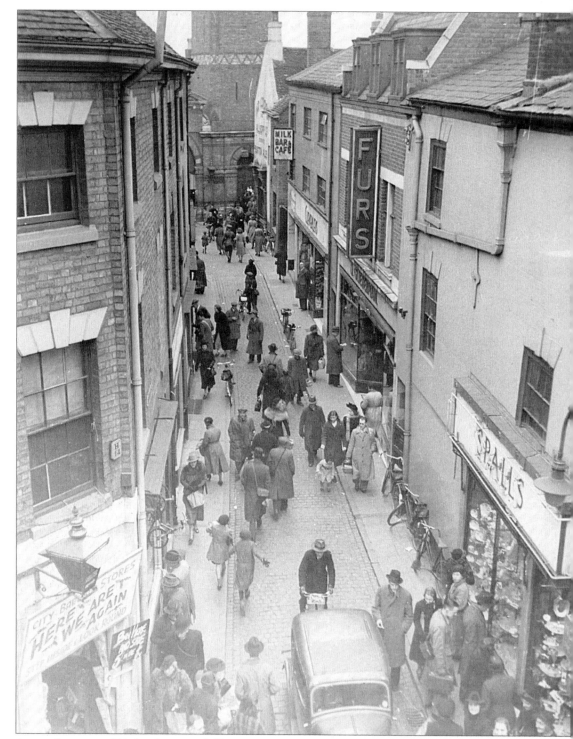

An excellent view of Market Street, probably *c*. 1939. Some people are carrying gas masks, a habit which quickly fell from favour as the 'Phoney War' got under way and the expected bombings didn't materialise. By the beginning of 1939, 232,000 respirators had been issued in the city.

THE RAIDS BEGIN, 1940

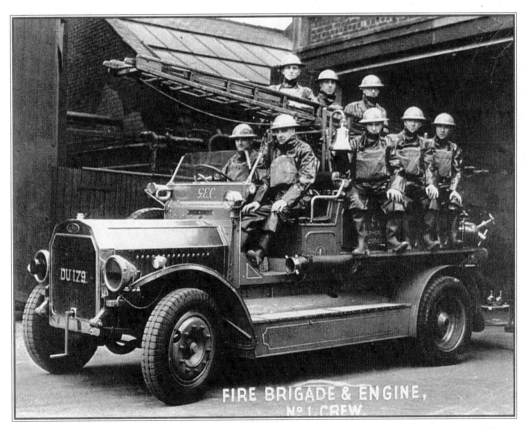

The crew of the GEC (General Electric Communications) company. GEC had been in Coventry since 1920; it produced munitions and VHF radio units for fighter defence. The engine is a fine vehicle, even then a museum piece.

Fire-fighter Arthur Day draining a static water tank near no. 6 entrance to the Humber Works in Stoke. Both the pump and the towing vehicle were scratch-built by the works in the early years of the war.

A rather austere-looking engine provided by the Home Office, a Fordson 7V, fitted with a 900 gallon per minute heavy pump. It was photographed at the rear of Hales Street central station in 1940.

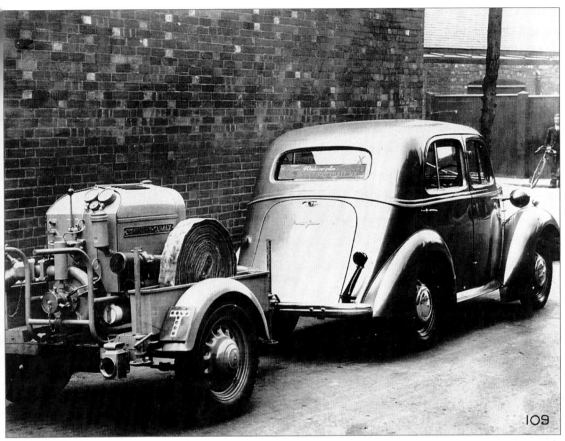

A Coventry Climax publicity photograph showing the lightness of the company's new FSM Trailer Pump. Its lightness meant it had no need for a specialist towing vehicle, and even a 'light' car such as this Vauxhall 10 could tow it. During petrol rationing vehicles such as the 10 could travel 40 miles to the gallon. This new pump was also portable, capable of being carried across debris to fires inaccessible to vehicles, and was considered invaluable to smaller district crews who could not be supplied with heavy appliances. Notice on the pump the pierced cylinder, behind the roll of hosepipe. This is the suction section which was dropped into the water supply. When used in canals or rivers a wicker basket was placed over this section to stop debris blocking the pump. John Bevan of Binley recalls his father dealing with such pumps during central station's weekly practice in Pool Meadow. He writes: 'The drill practice was to run with the pump to the River Sherbourne, drop the suction hose and basket into the river, which at that time was very low; then they had to run out four lengths of hose. . . . My father was in charge of one of the teams; he was given a place to draw water which looked impossible to do. The officer in charge was impressed with the way he achieved it . . . Father sent one of the team down to stand on the basket to keep it under the water.'

Firemen doing heavy respirator training somewhere in Coventry. Armed with their respirator, a hard hat and a torch these men were prepared to risk life and limb in burning properties.

Wartime vehicles parked at the camouflaged GEC plant. Behind the Climax fire appliances on the left can be seen an ambulance, no ordinary ambulance this but a Rolls-Royce. In the foreground are breathing apparatus cases and at either end foam tanks. These contained bulls' blood, which when mixed at high pressure with water created foam.

The old Hobart Motor Cycle Works at Cheylesmore, used by Coventry Climax to store completed fire pumps. The Climax's war production was based almost solely on these pumps, which were essential in protecting the Home Front.

A fascinating picture, as this 1922 tram has black-out paint and the word 'Coventry' removed from its side. This was done to all trams and buses after the evacuation at Dunkirk (ended 4 May 1940), because of the threat of invasion. All identifying names were removed throughout the land so as not to aid invading forces. Note the windows taped for bomb blast.

An aerial view of AWA Whitley plant, 1940. The site began as an airport created at the end of the First World War using the labour of locally held German prisoners of war. Armstrong Whitworth Aircraft took over the site in 1923 and began work on such things as the Atlas biplane. Note the barrage balloon, and that the site is criss-crossed with fake hedgerows painted on the ground.

The 25 August 1940 raid left this crater in Well Street. Note that despite the proximity of the crater there are but few broken panes of glass. Bombs were 'funny things', often taking the front off a house but leaving all inside untouched. My own father was blown from one side of Moseley Avenue to the other but walked away unhurt. Others, of course, were not so lucky.

The city's premier 2,550-seater theatre, the Rex, was opened in Corporation Street in 1937. This plush Philpot Circuit super cinema, built by Coventry's Philpot brothers, was struck by a single high explosive bomb on 25 August 1940 after the audience had left. Ironically the film due to be shown the following day was *Gone with the Wind*. Through the windows was the restaurant, mirrored and pillared and built around a tropical aviary.

It was planned after the August bombing to restore the Rex, but another raid in October put a stop to the plans when further bombs wrecked the foyer. Phillip Deeming recalls another night as he and his girlfriend left the cinema: 'searchlights were lighting the sky and it seemed very ominous. Hurrying on Binley Road we heard our first bombs dropping so we ran into a wooden garage. . . . Crouching on the floor, my girlfriend "laddered" her stockings – this was the tragedy of the evening as they were "on coupons".'

The final curtain falls on the Rex Cinema; too badly damaged to restore, it was demolished. Thus ended the short life of Coventry's super cinema.

Buses outside the Gas and Electric Showrooms in Corporation Street, autumn 1940. The showrooms, unlike the Rex opposite, survived the blitz, as did EWK 182 (Willenhall), which the inspector is looking at. The rear bus, EWK 240 (Coundon), was destroyed at the Keresley bus stop a few weeks after this picture was taken (see pages 45, 50 and 149).

October 1940 saw many raids on the city. These raids resulted in 176 deaths, 229 bad injuries and 451 minor injuries. The tram system took several hits, but these were quickly repaired. Here we see bus no. 254, a three-month-old bus flipped on its side by bomb blast in Pool Meadow, probably during the five hour raid that took place on 14 October. These raids were getting more serious, as the Revd G.W. Clitheroe wrote: 'The sirens sounded night after night.' Another vicar, the Revd Mr Sells of the now gone St Thomas's in the Butts, moved his family to Leamington on 15 October 1940 after his church was shaken by explosions on the previous evening. He, of course, returned, sleeping on a camp bed in the attic of the vicarage and taking a very active part in the protection of his area.

Ford's Hospital was founded by William Ford in 1509 in Greyfriars Lane to provide shelter to five aged men and one aged woman to 'look after their wants for evermore'. In 1517 William Pisford left money to increase the number of inmates. By the eighteenth century these inmates were exclusively female. For over 400 years life in the hospital was one of peace and quiet, but this was brought suddenly and violently to an end on 14 October 1940. On this night during a five hour raid a single bomb fell on the matron's room at the rear of the building. This resulted in the death of six inmates, the warden and nurse. It is noticeable in the photograph that the blast has blown off the roof, windows and has even damaged the building's sandstone base. Surprisingly the ancient technique of wattle and daub (twigs, mud, dung and hair) which fills the timber frame stood up to the ferocious blast. The destruction of Ford's Hospital brought to life some of the sites past for John Bailey Shelton, the father of Coventry's archaeology. Shelton explored the crater and found 'a number of encaustic tiles of the fourteenth century which must have formed the floor of a chapel. . . . One of these tiles was Earl Leofric's "Eagle", another was "Fleur de Leys". . . . A small piece of stone wall had also been left . . . suggesting that a stone building once stood here.' The building remained empty during the duration of the war and it was suggested by City Planner Donald Gibson that it be moved next to Bonds Hospital. The plan was not implemented, however, and the hospital was restored and re-opened in 1953, funded by Sir Alfred Herbert.

The Cranes Hotel was destroyed on the night of 12 October 1940. Of this event the Revd G.W. Clitheroe of Holy Trinity wrote: 'We had just passed the Cranes Hotel at the top of Bishop Street, and said goodnight to two police officers on duty there, when the scream of bombs caused us to take such cover as we could in shop fronts. When the explosions had ceased a cloud of dust hung over the road, the Cranes had gone, and the policemen (Sergeant Fox and P.C. Leadham) had been killed.' Also approaching the area was rescue man Albert Fearn (later awarded the George Medal); he wrote in his memoirs: 'As we neared the top of Bishop Street . . . a stick of bombs dropped in front of us . . . I just escaped decapitation by falling telephone wires. . . . I could see the Cranes public house had suffered a direct hit. Police Sergeant Fox had been killed and we were asked to go to a shelter . . . to check for casualties. . . . Next we were sent to Henry Street. . . . Here we had our first baptism of fire, realising the true horror of war. We went to a surface shelter . . . the whole roof came down on the poor people inside.'

These minor raids would lead to something worse for Hitler was infuriated as the RAF bombed Munich, the birthplace of Nazism. He yearned for revenge and Operation Moonlight Sonata was instigated. In the early evening of 14 November, 500 German bombers gathered. One squadron leader told his men: 'Our task is, with other squadrons, to repay the attack on Munich by the English during the night of 8 November. We shall not repay it in the same manner by smashing up harmless dwelling houses but we shall do it in such a way that those over there will be completely stunned . . . neither the Führer nor our Commander-in-Chief, Reichmarschell Goering, is willing to let even the attempt of an attack on the capital of the movement go unpunished, and we have therefore received orders to destroy the industries of Coventry tonight.' The night of the 'Big Raid' began.

THE 'BIG RAID'
& AFTER, 1940

Damage to the HumberWorks, Humber Road, November 1940. TheWorks continued producing cars during the war; these were, however, mainly for military use. The most famous was General Montgomery's Humber-Rootes staff car.

The night of 14 November started much like any other; the sky was clear and a full 'bomber's moon' shone down on the city. The bomber squadrons of General Field Marshals Kesselring and Sperrle, numbering over 500 planes, were following three radio beams which converged over the city. The first German planes (Kampfgeschwader 100), the 'pathfinders', were following these beams (called the X-Gerat System) using crude on-board computers. Soon in Coventry under the post office the 'war room' began tracking the approaching bombers, and at 7 p.m. the sirens sounded. Soon the droning of planes could be heard and by 7.20 p.m. the city's ack-ack burst forth as parachute flares hung like huge chandeliers over the city. With the arrival of the 'pathfinders' incendiaries began to fall, starting fires to mark the targets for the bombers that followed. At 7.30 p.m. the city began to shake as high explosives screamed down. Bombers crossed the city continuously, unloading their incendiaries, high-explosives, land-mines and oil-bombs every thirty seconds. Hundreds of fires turned into one great fire whipped up by a westerly wind. Flight-Sergeant Handor wrote of the event soon after: 'The Oberleutnant looks downwards. Their comrades' bombs still flash in the near and far neighbourhood; the streets . . . lie as bright as daylight beneath the aircraft. Dense smoke clouds billowing higher and higher. . . . Dark and almost smokeless flames stand here and there towering towards heaven. . . . A terrible beautiful picture of the most modern battle of destruction spreads before the airmen's gaze. . . . The flat cloud cover [which came over during the night] which still lies at about 10,000 feet . . . now assumed a red background. . . Hundreds of conflagrations characterised this unforgettable scene. Searchlights and the glowing path of tracers still flash almost invisible in the red reflection of the fires. Fresh hits flash in the distance as further waves of attacking aircraft arrive over their objectives.' The destruction continued for eleven long hours and blazing Coventry could be seen by bomber crews 150 miles away. The all-clear finally came at 6.15 a.m. the following morning. The Luftwaffe had unloaded 500 tons of high explosive bombs, 30,000 incendiaries and 50 land-mines on the city. Slowly the people emerged from their shelters to view the destruction. Here they stand in Broadgate. The Germans created a new word to describe the destruction – 'Coventrated'.

The east side of Broadgate with Holy Trinity Church in the background. On the left a single-decker bus doubles as an ambulance. The Revd G.W. Clitheroe wrote: 'From the battlements of Trinity Church the panorama might have been an illustration from Dante's *Inferno*. I could not believe then that anything had a chance of surviving. . . . I wondered how the dead would be buried!'

Firemen battle with a blaze still in progress in Hertford Street on the morning of 15 November. The November raid on Coventry was laid to create a fire-storm, and Coventry's fire-fighters were on the front-line in trying to control the inferno. The Chief Fire Officer's report tells of the events of the evening: 'The yellow message was received at 1905 . . . the red at 1910. . . . The first fire was reported at 19.24. . . . Fifty-six calls were recorded in the first half hour. . . . By now [19.59] seventy-one calls had been received and all the local pumps were in action. The intensity of the action increased . . . the attack was of an unprecedented nature . . . incendiary bombs, explosives, oil bombs, HEs of all calibres, parachute mines and flares were all being used. . . . Outside aid was arriving . . . fires were started in the roof of the Headquarters Station . . . it became necessary to abandon the control room. . . . Reports of water shortage . . . static supplies in use . . . dams in Sherbourne used. . . . Swimming and ornamental pools . . . into full operation. Supplies from the canal . . . utilised until hit by HE. . . . At 20.47 telephones out of order. . . . At 23.15 forty more pumps asked for. . . . By now the position was critical. . . . Outside assistance was held up by road blockages. . . . The fires in the centre of the City combine to make a single incident . . . the spread of fire was checked. . . . Fatigued and under continual bombardment, they [the fire-fighters] worked incessantly. . . . In many cases after fires had been dealt with pumps had to be abandoned owing to being hemmed in by debris and wrecked buildings . . . many fires were not reported . . . being dealt with by police, wardens, other services and civilians.' After a long night of bravery twenty-six fire-fighters lay dead; thirty-four were seriously injured and two hundred suffered minor injuries. Indeed it was a miracle that more were not killed.

Looking across Broadgate at the Market Clock on the morning of 15 November. Many made their way to work, only to find that their place of work no longer existed.

The morning of 15 November; the city is shrouded in fog, a mixture of smoke and drizzle. People walk down what remains of Cross Cheaping. Owen Owen stands on the right completely gutted by incendiaries; the shop also acted as a shelter, having a deep basement entered via Palmer Lane. A group of fire-fighters were killed

beside Owen Owen when a land-mine blew a building down upon them as they fought to contain the fire which was engulfing Owen Owen. Despite their smashed pumps and dead colleagues the firemen recovered another pump from the bottom of Cross Cheaping and continued their work.

Little Park Street, 15 November. During the conflagration that destroyed the street a Home Guard motor-cycle messenger recalled how the fires were so intense that they met in the middle of the road. These would have trapped him had he not escaped across a car-park into Cheylesmore. Coventry's amateur archaeologist J.B. Shelton lived in Little Park Street and wrote of the night in a booklet entitled 'A Night in Little Park Street': 'The entry from my yard to the street had two large doors. . . . I opened them and went into the street, finding the old Swift cycle factory, now storehouse and printers press, etc., well alight and a fireman attaching his water pipes to the hydrant. . . . As I returned to the stables high explosive bombs began to fall every half-minute or so and made the ground and sheds seem to leap in the air. . . . Small fires became larger ones until they joined and were a four or five acre flame. . . . The factory walls girders, pillars, machinery crashing four storeys. The droning of the planes as they let go of their bombs and the rattling of shrapnel on corrugated sheeting was deafening.' The crashing 'four storeys' came from Bushill's Printers, which stood on the right of the photograph. The makeshift barrier was placed across the street because of an unexploded bomb; no one was allowed past this point.

People walk up and down Cross Cheaping as if unaware of the destruction around them. Among this unreality soldiers toured the streets, picking up body parts and putting them in sacks.

One of the many hundreds of troops drafted into the city stands in Jordan Well, near the corner of Much Park Street. Armed troops were sent in as it was assumed chaos would ensue in the destroyed city; the problem did not materialise, however.

People gather on the north-east side of Broadgate (by the lane to Holy Trinity Church). The makeshift barrier probably indicates that earlier the area was blocked because of a UXB. A policeman watches the people as an armed soldier passes by. Above the ladder (by the lamppost) hangs a union jack, one of many put up after the

bombing. A commercial traveller who often visited the city later wrote: 'having got over the initial shock, I think they are now prepared to stand anything.'

Residents of St George's Road standing on the edge of a bomb crater on the morning of 15 November. Six houses were destroyed including the home of the Hammond family. Mrs A. Hammond and her sons, Martyn and Bryan, can be seen (front right). Martyn (holding the bundle) recalled the 'scream of the bomb' and the blast through the brick street air raid shelter they were hiding in. As they sought protection elsewhere the ruins of their home was looted, Martyn recalls: 'Three bicycles disappeared from the garden shed and a load of coal mother had stored up during the summer. . . . My bicycle was pretty new which I had bought from Pollards and was paying for each week from my paper round job.' The Hammond family of six children was split between relatives in Middlesex and Essex. Martyn spent time at Ilford outside London, where 'the air-raid sirens went nearly every night . . . out of the frying pan into the fire.'

Cross Cheaping, 15 November. As the city still smouldered hundreds of troops were drafted in to help and keep order. The Government worried that panic and looting would ensue, but these fears were unfounded – only two arrests were made for looting during the height of the bombing. Meanwhile the army, the rescue services and the people dug through the rubble in search of survivors.

Jordan Well, midday 15 November. Two shops lie on each side, literally blown into the road. Nearby Bayley Lane lay under 4 ft of rubble. Some shops in Jordan Well opened as usual despite the destruction, including the tobacconist who continued trading with 'half a shop.'

Bus EWK 240 for Coundon lies smashed in Cross Cheaping on the morning of Friday 15 November 1940. Out of 181 buses only 73 remained undamaged. Despite this a service was under way on the 16th. With the partial destruction of the fleet, buses were brought in from all over the country.

A wrecked Riley Kestrel outside the rubble that was previously Boots the Chemist in Broadgate. The vehicle was towed away by its owner and restored to roadworthiness by the Riley Works: it is still in use today.

Early morning on the 15th and people pick their way through the smoke-filled city streets.

Looking down Cross Cheaping from the bottom of Broadgate on the morning of 15 November. People wander the destroyed city in a daze to talk and view the destruction.

Looking across a shattered Smithford Street towards the Market Square and West Orchard, probably on 16 November.

Bomb damage at the Central Fire Station was caused on 14–15 November. The Chief Fire Officer's report reads: 'To add to the difficulty of operation, fires were started in the roof . . . [and] it became necessary to abandon the Control Room. Water from these fires caused the switchboard to become "alive", and by 20.00 all the lines . . . were out of order. The main lighting failed and the emergency lighting was badly affected.'

Early morning in lower Broadgate, 15 November. Smoke still hangs in the air because of the drizzle. The rubble on the left (corner of the Market Place) was until a few hours earlier a tobacconist. Its store-room of tobacco can still be seen 'smoking' at the rear.

Two police officers walk down Much Park Street on 15 November. The car in the crater belonged to the son of the landlady of the Greyhound in Much Park Street. He was killed when the bomb landed and he crashed into the crater. The car's passenger spent the night of the 14th–15th wandering the streets in a daze. Much Park Street would suffer again in the April 1941 raids. The only remaining building in this picture is Whitefriars Gate in the centre.

Burnt out buildings and rubble line Vicar Lane and Market Street on 15 November, framing the market clock next to the remains of the market. In the middle of this rubble lies Smithford Street.

The destruction of Coventry had shocked the world but what shocked many even more was the destruction of the cathedral of St Michael. On the night of its destruction, 14 November, the Revd R.T. Howard, Jack Forbes the stonemason and two younger men, Mr White and Mr Eaton, were on duty protecting the building. The men were on the roof of the building when the first incendiary hit at about 7.40 p.m. The fire brigade were called, but soon more incendiaries fell and the group fought to control them as they burnt through the lead roof falling into the 18-in roof space. Lead had to be ripped up to find the fires, which were close to taking hold on the old timbers. As one string of bombs was dealt with they were quickly replaced by more. Soon things were getting out of hand. Four incendiaries that had landed above the Girdlers Chapel by the north door in the north aisle burned through and took hold before the desperate fire-fighters could get to them. The north aisle was in flames, more incendiaries fell and the men realised they were fighting a losing battle. They climbed down off the roof and tried to save what they could in the smoke-filled interior. They then waited by the south porch amid the explosions, watching history burned by gigantic red flames, and waited in desperation for the fire service. At 9.30 a group of firemen from Solihull had battled their way through to the cathedral and quickly set up their hoses. As the water hit the red-hot roof huge pillars of steam rose. Hope did not last, for within a short time the water stopped as the mains was hit. On the nave and south aisle a policeman and soldier were throwing off incendiaries despite the roof burning around them. Their heroism had to stop, however, when the policeman was injured by an exploding incendiary, a device first used by the Germans on this raid. Work continued to save items from the interior and at 10.30 the firecrew had managed to hook up another hose; this, however, suffered the same fate as the first, and nothing more could be done except let Coventry's pride burn.

This excellent photograph shows Coventrians passing the remains of Coventry's Reference Library in Cuckoo Lane. The Revd G.W. Clitheroe in his booklet 'Coventry Under Fire' wrote of the library's destruction as he fought to save Holy Trinity Church. He wrote: 'we saw the City Library . . . was alight. This too was lamentable, for we knew how precious were its contents, and how much they meant to us in Coventry. . . . Once again, could we dare dash across. . . . But no! Down came an incendiary in the Archdeacon's Court.'

Practically all the mains in the city centre were destroyed and water had to be brought in from outside. Water from any surviving supply had to be boiled, just in case. Here we see survivors carrying water past Judges Court in Little Park Street.

Members of the Home Guard dealing with the horrors of war in a Coventry street, possibly in Radford. The truck in the background will carry away the remnants of another life.

Looking across Broadgate from Hertford Street on the morning of 15 November 1940.

The same view a few years earlier in 1936. Some of these buildings date back to at least the sixteenth century.

Eagle Street, Foleshill, on the morning of 15 November. In the foreground are Albert and Elizabeth Asplin outside their home, now a pile of rubble. They survived the night in their Anderson shelter in the back garden. The buildings

to the left were hit by a string of high explosives and later had to be demolished.

Rescue Service men searching for survivors amongst the rubble in the general area of Pool Meadow. It took a speci
kind of persistence to dig through tons and tons of rubble, hour after hour, in search of possible survivors. One suc
man was Albert Fearn, and he recorded his feelings at the time: 'I fear that sometimes I was getting quite callous, mor
used to looking at violent death in the face.' He recalled two young women dressed to the nines on a Friday night, or
still clutching her powder compact, both dead in a shelter. Albert remembered: 'I was left alone with the bodies. N
marks or blemishes on their faces, just a substance coming out of their ears, which told it was the blast that had kille
them. It made me feel so sad. . . . I am still haunted by the look on their faces, eyes wide with shock.' Clearing rubble t
find bodies or burrowing tiny tunnels through the rubble stuck in Albert's mind. He wrote: 'If you can imagine
mixture of broken bricks, mortar, furniture, laths, joists, broken glass and lumps of concrete, all mixed up with broke
and bent pipes. Then there is leaking water or gas, along with broken cutlery, crockery, pots and pans and othe
household equipment, all enveloped in thick plaster, dust and the smell of wet plaster and gas. That was rubble.' Alber
Fearn was awarded the George Medal in 1941.

Part of the art of rescue was
listening quietly for any
sounds of survival, while
deciding how the rescue could
be successfully carried out.
Someone would have to go in.

Work begins on clearing rubble halfway down bombed-out Smithford Street.

A 1,000-lb 'Herman' bomb, nicknamed thus because it was large and fat, not unlike Reichsmarshal Herman Goering. This particular bomb fell on the Embodiment Store of the Bristol Aero Engine Repair Section of the Humber works in Stoke. It buried itself 9 ft below the ground and remained unexploded. A Bomb Disposal Unit opened the massive bomb and steam-pumped 20 cwt of high explosive out of it. Then the 9 ft 6 in bomb was hoisted out of the crater, tidied up and put on display in the factory. It now stands in Coventry's Museum of British Road Transport. By the end of the war the disposal units of the Royal Engineers had dealt with 527 unexploded bombs in the city, while a further 16 blew up before they could be properly disposed of. Bombs which could not be dealt with on the spot were taken to Whitley Common and blown up. One such duty went disastrously wrong when on 18 October 1940 a 500 pounder was removed from Chapel Street and exploded as it was being unloaded, killing some of the men of No. 9 unit. Marty Hammond, then a young boy, recalled visiting the common. He wrote: 'One day in school we heard a large explosion which we knew to be a delayed bomb being set off on Whitley Common. We gathered from local talk that the soldiers were about to lift it off the lorry when it detonated. After school a group of us went to the common and walked around. It was a gruesome scene with bits of men hanging from the trees and bushes, with parts of their uniforms and the lorry strewn all over. We were surprised that the area wasn't cordoned off and we children allowed to wander around. My brother picked up a piece of a soldier's web belt and brought it home.' This was the great threat to the UXB men; how do you tell a DA (Delayed Action) bomb from one that has simply failed to go off? The brave crew of No. 9 unit were buried together at the London Road Cemetery; two posthumously received the George Cross.

Broadgate still smoking a couple of days after the raid. Holy Trinity Church towers above the remains of the east side of Broadgate. The clock stopped at 10.40 p.m. on the night of 14 November. Below it can be seen broken fire hoses which were blown apart as firemen fought to control the conflagration.

Two members of the Home Guard carry Peeping Tom into Hertford Street. Luckily the fifteenth-century figure had been removed from his fourth-storey nook well before the outbreak of war. As the King's Head was destroyed Tom had to be removed to a place of great safety. He therefore spent the remainder of the war years in the vault of the nearby bank.

Clearance well underway by Royal Engineers in Earl Street. Among the rubble on the right was one of Coventry's finest buildings, namely the sixteenth-century Palace Yard, destroyed by a single high-explosive. The Council House (left) survived but had all of its windows smashed. James Taylor wrote in the *Coventry Standard* of the damage: 'In front of the Council House all the property was ablaze. . . . The [Council] staff were busy removing papers to the basement and when I called on the Town Clerk [Frederick Smith, Coventry historian] who was an ardent Coventrian, I found him in tears.' Civil Defence Officer Howard Tomley wrote, 'I proceeded along Jordan Well into Earl Street. There was a body of a youth lying on the pavement just underneath the Council House clock; he was dead. Later I heard he was one of the brave body of police messengers.'

A Ministry of Information van tours the city giving advice about where food could be obtained and help for th
homeless. With 4,330 houses destroyed and thousands damaged, indeed there were many homeless. Between 1931 and
1940 Coventry's population had increased by about 110,000. Housing had not increased so war-workers were boarded
in private homes (by 1941, 25,000 in lodgings). To help, the council had to build large hostel complexes in places such
as Keresley and Willenhall. After the 'Big Raid' the city was in a terrible state. The Women's Voluntary Service, Salvation
Army and the YMCA opened twenty-nine relief stations handing out food and clothes. Several field army kitchens and
seventeen mobile canteens toured the streets; even cafés opened as unofficial soup kitchens. Temporary mains were laid
with the aid of the Royal Engineers and within three days electricity had been restored to most of the city. Water and
gas quickly followed, and the threat of typhoid from dirty water was combated by the inoculation of 100,000
individuals. One unforeseen problem was that people could only get food from shops for which they held ration books,
unfortunately 624 shops had been destroyed so the whole system needed revision. Philip Deeming of Allesley Park
remembers the problems caused by the 'Big Raid': 'The raid left us with no water or gas, but the GEC brought in
Bowsers and allowed the local residents to fetch fresh water from them until the mains were repaired. Unfortunately
the gas supply took longer and cooking had to be carried out as best as possible; on the open coal fire.' Coventry soon
had its vital services restored, as Coventry's war production was vital to the war effort.

A homeless woman wanders the streets
with her most important surviving
possessions, her children.

Coventry station was hit by nine high explosive bombs. Two failed to explode: one of these landed in the main booking
hall and the other in the taxi rank. The ones that exploded destroyed 50 yd of track and platform and two rail coaches.

A turntable ladder attended by its crew in Broadgate. Such devices were few and far between in the city and were only available to the city's established fire brigade.

Looking down Cross Cheaping a few days after the 'Big Raid'. The wrecked lorry and EWK 240 have been removed as the clearance gets underway. On the left in the background can be seen the gutted Rover factory.

People gather to purchase the salvaged remains of a bombed shop's stock, a scene not uncommon in the devastated city centre.

George VI rushed to devastated Coventry on 16 November, to see for himself the destruction, with the mayor, Alderman J.A. Moseley (second from right), Herbert Morrison, the Home Secretary and Minister for Home Security (left), and Coventry's Chief Constable, Captain S.A. Hector (far right). The king spent four hours walking the shattered streets. He later wrote in his diary: 'I walked among the devastation. The people in the streets wondered where they were, nothing could be recognised . . . the town looks just like Ypres after the last war.'

The King walks up Broadgate. Behind stands Owen Owen. During his visit the king saw much, ranging from the cathedral to the small house of the mayor in Kensington Road. He ended the tour with a cold buffet in the Council House.

People gather around the list of casualties pinned on a board in Hay Lane at the side of the Council House. Above it, hurriedly scrawled in chalk, are the words 'Enquiries re. casualties on top floor, re. deaths on first floor.' Eileen Castle in her booklet, 'The City Under Fire', cites an event which directly relates to this scene. It reads: 'I was in Hay Lane, by the corner of Anslows. There was a queue of people trying to get some news of relatives who were dead or missing. Without any warning the King suddenly appeared, in army uniform. He was walking with a group of people and I always remember a bus conductor who climbed a gas-lamp post and clung on to it and waved his hat in the air shouting, "Three cheers for King George!" It was quite marvellous!'

The Humber Works produced many war vehicles including staff cars and scout cars. These were so reliable that Field Marshal Rommel used a captured Humber scout car for his desert campaigns. The works received a number of direct hits on the night of the 'Big Raid'. Here we see men salvaging the service stores.

Clearing the damage caused on the night of 14–15 November. A limited production re-started within two days and the factory returned to full production within two months. Little did the workmen in this photograph realise that the building to the left of them contained a large delayed action bomb, waiting to go off. Note the entrance to the Planning Department – and see the next photo.

It is now 17 November, and the DA has exploded – completely flattening the building seen in the previous photograph.
Such bombs were highly dangerous as they often exploded while clearance was under way. This particular bomb
resulted in the deaths of several workers who, as in the previous shot, were clearing the wreckage.

shop completely
gutted by fire, probably
caused by phosphorus
incendiary bombs.
The heat has twisted the
building's roof beams
totally out of
recognition.

Bomb damage sustained at the Humber Service Stores, Humber Road factory, 16 November 1940.

Men search through the remains of an office which until recently had occupied the City Arcade off Smithford Street. One man has discovered a typewriter, but little else appears salvageable in this part of the building. The glass panelled arcade roof was not surprisingly smashed.

The end of a terrace of houses in Treherne Road, Radford.
In the background can be seen Burnaby Road. A Voluntary Rescue Squad from Motor Panels reported that 'We arrived at Treherne Road just as large quantities of landmines were being dropped . . . one of the squad had to shoot a dog that was in bad condition. . . . A number of people had been killed. . . .'

The Philpot Circuit Savoy Cinema and ballroom, Radford Road, had its roof blown off on 14 November. Opposite, St Nicholas' Church was flattened by a single land-mine, an event witnessed by my father. As the church was destroyed the ballroom of the Savoy was used for a short time for Sunday services. The building was hit again in the Easter raids of 1941, but re-opened in September.

The children's paddling pool on the Binley Road after a direct hit from a small bomb. Larger bombs, such as the 1,000-lb 'Herman', made craters big enough for a bus to fit in. One such crater was produced at the bottom of Cox Street.

The original church of St Francis of Assisi in Links Road, Radford (now the church hall). The roof had been blasted off but the cross remained untouched. The church was restored, and my parents married there in December 1945.

One Coventrian cheerily salvages what he can from his damaged home. In an uncertain world material things could lose their significance as long as one survived.

The Market Clock Tower, a local landmark built in 1867, stands starkly against the spires of Holy Trinity Church (left) and St Michael's (right). After the raids untrue rumours began to circulate that there were so many dead bodies under the Market Hall that it would just be sealed up. These rumours prompted an official denial in the *Midland Daily Telegraph* on 25 November to stop the rumours spreading; it didn't work.

Coventrians wander the ruins of the cathedral, which only a short time before had been 'a sea of seething flames . . . and bronze coloured smoke'. Smashed to pieces below the rubble lay tombs of knights and ladies. In the Lady Chapel to the left of the east window one tomb survived; the tomb that bore the reclining figure of the cathedral's first bishop, Yeatman-Biggs.

Looking through what was the great west door; solid Warwickshire oak turned to ash, leaving the fifteenth-century iron hinges hanging in mid-air. Those who wandered the ruins were not all Coventrians, for hundreds came from all around to witness the destruction. In the background can be seen the east window, once full of fifteenth-century glass, which had been removed and stored at Hampton Lucy before the outbreak of war.

A fine drawing of the ruined St Michael's and spire of Holy Trinity Church. In the foreground (right) can be seen the Provost, the Very Revd R.T. Howard, and the cathedral's stonemason, Jack Forbes. Jack was responsible for the famed charred cross, which he made by binding two charred timbers together with wire and planting them amongst the rubble.

Looking west down the stark ruins of Coventry Cathedral. The metal bands in the foreground were bolted to the main roof beams in the 1885–90 restoration. The expansion and twisting of these metal bands during the roof fire led to the complete internal collapse of the building.

This photograph, taken on 17 November, shows the shell of Owen Owen standing on the right, burnt out by incendiaries. The store had suffered in an earlier raid when a high explosive bomb plunged through the roof and exploded on the ground floor. The building was to be repaired but nothing could stop its final destruction on 14 November. Cross Cheaping is cleared as lorries are loaded with rubble from the wrecked shops on the west of the street.

Men work on restoring damaged houses on the Scotchill, Keresley, 1940. Hundreds of builders were brought into the city as much repair work was needed. By the end of the war 56,373 houses were damaged and 3,882 completely destroyed. Within five weeks of the November raid 12,000 homes had been repaired and work continued at over 500 a day. Houses beyond repair were cannibalised to repair those in better condition.

Looking west past Owen Owen towards West Orchard and the Market Square as trucks carry away rubble. Harry Ward of the Bell Inn, Keresley, wrote in 1942 in *The City We Loved* his memory of the November raid, as he, his wife and daughter tried to escape their burning hotel. He wrote: 'The scene was a terrifying one . . . we beat a hasty retreat . . . through the burning hotel . . . into the Market Square. The roar of planes, the crash of bombs, the fierce flames, and the scorching heat made our position seem hopeless, but the crash of the bursting petrol tank of a burning bus in the Market Square lent speed to our bodies as we made for Broadgate.'

The mass burial of victims of the 'Big Raid' on 14 November, taking place on 20 November 1940. This section of th
London Road Cemetery had to be put aside for the inevitable victims of air-raids. This is the first of two mass burials
Soldiers and grave-diggers were brought in by the bus-load to work overnight, digging two long trenches and fillin
them with 172 plain oak coffins, two deep, draped with union jacks. The Revd Leslie Cook wrote of the event: 'So on
grey November day we gathered in the cemetery. . . . The service for the Anglicans and Free Churchmen . . . wa
combined . . . preceded by a service . . . by the Roman Catholic Priests. . . . In the background stood the mechanica
trench-digger and groups of soldiers and labourers. . . . The Bishop of Coventry and the clergy and ministers, the Mayo
and civic officials . . . stood about in groups. . . . They all looked strained and tired . . . for each of them . . . had bee
dealing with suffering and death . . . the Bishop and clergy took the lead. . . . In the distance against the grey scuddin
sky, a Spitfire wheeled and twisted . . . it was possible to turn back over the long line of mourners . . . women carryin
wreaths . . . a child with a bunch of flowers. . . . It seemed as if there was no end to this dark line. . . .' While thi
ceremony was proceeding, bodies were still being discovered in the ruins of the city. The following Saturday anothe
250 citizens were buried, and more was to come. Officially over the war years 1,236 were killed in Coventry; 808 o
them rest in the London Road Cemetery. Others who came into the city for war-work were taken back home fo
burial. Others were never found.

The old church in Holbrook Lane opened in 1916 for munition workers, and was used in the early 1940s as a refuge for those who had lost their homes. The windows are painted out, or blasted out in a recent raid. Note the font in the background.

St Luke's new church (opened 1938) suffered badly from bomb damage in December 1940, and was not re-opened until October 1944.

The Auxiliary Fire Service crew of Station 605 photographed outside their base at the London Laundry, 1940. They served the Stoney Stanton Road area known locally as 'Hellfire Corner.' Three members of 605 were killed while helping others, and their station too fell to the bombs, leaving them to work from the house of one of the crew.

Smiling members of Station 605 pose around their fire apparatus, a Hillman Minx, on the Stoney Stanton Road. The church (now disused) can be seen in the background.

MORE RAIDS,
AWA & CHURCHILL, 1941

Temporary shops designed by city architect Donald Gibson under construction on the corner of Hill and Corporation Street, 24 February 1941. The shops, made of bricks, clay blocks and asbestos, had small windows to minimise damage from bomb blast. Despite being temporary the shops were in use until their demolition in June 1995. Behind can be seen buildings lining Bond Street.

Trams standing in the Foleshill depot, 1941. Their black-out markings and lamp shades are still intact but these vehicle were no longer in use. Coventry Transport had already agreed to phase out trams by 1942, replacing them with buse. The night of 14–15 November 1940 left the tram system in disarray; no trams were destroyed but the system th. supported it, mainly the lines and overhead wires, was smashed. Steel tram lines were thrown through the air, landir in people's gardens and even through roofs; others were twisted out of shape *in situ*. The Foreman of Coventr Tramways Department made a tour of the city the morning after and wrote: 'The power cables had been ripped ou during the raid and left trams standing where they were. . . . All had to be towed back to the depot. . . . I found tra lines ripped up, craters everywhere . . . in places the rails were standing up to twenty to thirty feet in the air . . . a lad came . . . and said, "There is part of a tram line on our back lawn." I went to find out what it was . . . a complet crossing complete with sets . . . the whole thing would weigh about fifteen cwt. . . . It had been blown over a thre storey house . . . and took five men to move it. . . . An old lady came to me . . . she said, "There's a piece of tram line o my son's bed." I found a piece of tram rail about twelve feet long. . . . A caretaker . . . asked us to clear his school yarc We had a load of sets and rails from there, yet it was a good quarter of a mile from the nearest track.' Not surprising the system came to an early end.

Clearing rubble from the blasted Coventry and Warwickshire Hospital on the morning of 9 April 1941. Matron Joyce Burton described the scene: 'a bomb fell directly in front of the Enquiry Office making a large crater . . . this lifted those standing with me . . . through the double doorway . . . the end wall of both this and the next floor had been blown away . . . windows were blown out but the wards were lit by the fires outside.'

Joyce Burton, hospital matron and George Medal holder, recalled this scene which was photographed on 9 April 1941 the morning after a heavy raid: 'The patients had previously been put under the beds . . . we did a complete tour with a torch looking under each bed. . . . During this time the top floor on the other side of the building had received a direct hit. . . . We went to investigate and found that an ambulance had been lifted by the blast of a bomb up on the top of the balcony [15 ft up]. Had our troubles ceased then I think we should have considered ourselves fortunate.' The old hospital was almost totally destroyed during this raid – two doctors, nine nurses, two porters and twenty patients were killed. Four members of staff were awarded the George Medal.

The shell and fourteenth-century tower and spire of Christchurch, late 1941. Christchurch was destroyed by incendiaries on 8–9 April 1941. This was the second body of the church to be destroyed, the first being demolished during the Dissolution in the sixteenth century. Originally the church of the Greyfriars Friary, it was rebuilt in 1832; as the land on the east side could not be acquired its altar stood most unusually underneath the tower arch.

The ruins of the seventeenth-century Grapes Inn in Hertford Street, photographed on the morning of 9 April 1941. Behind, stands Christchurch. The raids of 8 and 10 April were the most intense since 14 November raid. Some claim that these raids were in fact worse than the 'Big Raid'. Note the 'Keep Left' sign hooded to conform to black-out regulations.

Houses in Cheveral Avenue, Radford, damaged by bombs in April 1941. Note the upper windows are taped against bomb blast. As glass was unobtainable broken windows were replaced by a semi-transparent canvas-type material.

Rosehill, on the site of the present Coachmakers Club on the Radford Road, blasted by bomb damage. This was the home of Thomas Cash of weaving fame, built on the site of the previous Rosehill, home of Charles Bray and second home of novelist George Eliot.

The Stonehouse in Much Park Street,
1941. This rare stone fourteenth-
century merchant's house was
discovered after the April raids, when
bomb blast threw down part of the
brickwork which had encased the
building, hiding it for centuries.

The complete wartime crew of the Stoke National Fire Service station based at Stoke Park School in Dane Road.
By August 1941 all local fire brigades were absorbed into the National Fire Service.

Firemen testing hoses against the old Meteor Works in West Orchard, 1941. As wartime hoses were rubberised canvas they needed to be hung and dried after use. The Central Fire Station in Hales Street had a hose drying tower which doubled as a watch-out tower. This was bombed out of action in autumn 1940. The hoses were thereafter dried at the Courtaulds plant.

The crew of the NFS station at Jubilee Crescent, Radford. The station was based within the shops, the left bay in the photo now being the long established Godiva Fish Bar. Jubilee Crescent also had a trench shelter capable of holding 306 people. The concrete entrance to the shelter can still be seen in the middle of the green.

Morris Engines, Courthouse Green: not the works fire brigade, but the First Aid and Breathing Apparatus crew posing before their firm's fire appliance with their newly acquired trophy.

Barry Palmer of Cheylesmore standing on the rear step of a Dennis pump-ladder appliance. Young Barry was the mascot of Cheylesmore National Fire Service crew. The station was based at the Daventry Buildings shops.

GEC fire crew on the roof of the Spon Street factory (now gone) with a Climax pump. Note the tower of St John's in the background.

Rescue workers in training at a mock building, probably at Styvechale, early 1940s. Their skills and persistence was put to good use on the city centre and suburbs.

A set of cartoons from Van Art's wartime local best-seller, *Going To It*. Van Art was Coventry-born Arthur Keene wh worked for Riley Cars at Dunbar Avenue painting number plates and monograms. He also created Riley mascots including their famous skiing lady which graced the bonnet of all Riley cars. Arthur also produced work for the company's magazine, including coloured drawings of Rileys racing at Brooklands which sold nationally as prints. H produced many fine paintings during his lifetime, but above all he is remembered for his cartoons. During the grim wa years Van Art cartoons brought a smile to many a face, not just locally, but nationally. Twenty thousand copies of *Going To It* were ordered, but the paper needed to produce them was unobtainable as it was wartime. Arthur lived his latter year at Meriden; painting, giving after dinner speeches, entertaining, generally making people smile. He died in 1986.

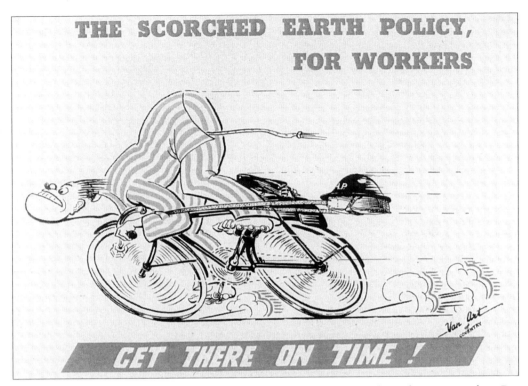

'Getting there on time' was important during wartime as lateness could lead to a fine. One Auxiliary Fire Service man who worked at Ryton had to cycle home, have his tea and spend all evening on duty; when one day he was late for work he was fined. Well, that's war for you.

'The Spirit of Britain' reflected the determination of the British people to carry on, come what may.

Broadgate and beyond from St Michael's tower, 1941. Most rubble has been cleared but some still remains. On the south of Broadgate stands the Burton Building (demolished January 1948) and (left) Martins Bank, which began life as a Georgian town house; later it became tea and coffee merchants, Atkins and Turton. It was demolished in 1990 during the building of Cathedral Lanes. As the centre was destroyed 2,464 shops had to be relocated, and the rationed shoppers of 1941 had to walk longer distances for their foodstuffs.

After the evacuation of the British army from Dunkirk in the summer of 1940 the Government decided to form citizen's army to defend the Home Front against invasion, especially airborne attack. The new army of young and ol men was first called the Local Defence Volunteers. Initially they were ill equipped and made their own weapons. Som shared one rifle between five, but as time passed, with improved training and better equipment, the men who wer now known as the Home Guard really could make a difference. John Stanton recalls the role of his father, Willian Stanton, as a member of the Home Guard: 'Dad would spend a couple of evenings or so each week [on Home Guard duties], and again on Sunday; like most people he was working six days a week so it was quite a sacrifice. Sometimes h would be away on Saturday night as well on night manoeuvres. He took on the position of Gas Corporal within hi platoon and was responsible for all the anti-gas equipment. His platoon was based at his place of work, Humber Ltd and was part of the Royal Warwickshire Regiment (Home Guard). The TV series "Dads Army" was a jolly good laugh but it was a very serious business at the time.' When the Home Guard disbanded in 1944 it consisted of over tw million men. The photograph shows William Stanton (back right) with other members of his platoon at the Humbe Works. Note the bomb damage in the background, and also the semi-transparent material used to replace blasted glass.

The Humber Home Guard enjoy a social occasion at their base in the works cricket pavilion, Humber Road Recreation Ground. Note in the background the permanent aeroplane recognition display – a case of 'know your enemy.'

Part of the Humber Works Home Guard posing outside their cricket pavilion base, next to a section of the camouflaged factory.

A Whitley bomber flying over the edge of Coventry. The Whitley, built and designed in Coventry at the original Armstrong Whitworth Aircraft (AWA) factory at Whitley, was the first heavy bomber used in the Second World War. It was initially designed for the Czech Government, but was later accepted by the Air Ministry who ordered two in 1934. The first prototype flew from Whitley on 16 March 1936; two months later AWA's Baginton works came into use. In 1935 work began on eighty Whitleys with Tiger engines. By 1937 the bomber was already outdated and new types were developed bearing greater bomb-loads. At the outbreak of war the Whitley had been perfected with the Mark V, featuring both tail and nose gun turrets. The Whitley was the first British bomber to penetrate German airspace when they dropped propaganda leaflets in September 1939. Soon afterwards it was on regular heavy bombing missions and became the work-horse of the RAF. Other work included U-boat hunting, carrying paratroops and pulling troop gliders. By June 1943 Bomber Command had received 1,466 Whitley Vs; none now survive.

Churchill outside the main camouflaged Flight Sheds at AWA's works during his visit to Coventry in September 1941.

Churchill heads back to the factory after watching the fly-over of a Whitley bomber.

By 1943 three million married women and widows were engaged nationally on war-work. Here in the Armstrong Whitworth factory women literally did work shoulder to shoulder in this packed machine shop full of lathes.

Two women riveting the shell of a Whitley bomber.

A young lady engaged in more detailed work on the bomber's airframe.

Riveting the fuselage of a bomber. Of the local workforce at AWA 60 per cent were women; some were local but many were brought in by bus from Nuneaton, Leicester and Northampton.

Riveting the Whitley body-frame. All Whitley
bomber fuselages were produced at AWA's
Whitley Abbey works. Each bomber needed
thousands of rivets, each placed in a 'dolly'
and 'domed.'

Drilling holes for rivets in the body of
a Whitley bomber.

Two young ladies drilling a tail section of a Lancaster bomber at the Baginton factory.

One of AWA's three bay assembly sheds at Baginton. The first complete Baginton Whitley, the Whitley IV complete with Merlin engines, was flown from the Baginton site on 18 April 1939.

The final assembly bay at AWA, showing Whitley bombers nearing completion. During the period March 1937 to June 1943 the works produced and sent into combat 1,812 Whitley bombers from this hangar.

'The Sting of a Whitley': AWA's float for the War Bonds campaign. Mounted on a Ford truck is a Whitley tail gun-turret with its 'sting', the 303 Browning machine gun.

A front view of the AWA War Bonds, V for Victory float, complete with black-out markings and light covers.

Looking across West Orchard, across Smithford Street. Thousands of tons of rubble have been cleared away. American Ernie Pile, correspondent for the *Boston Sunday Globe*, wrote: 'As a friend of mine said, "There are probably more secondhand bricks here today than anywhere else in the world." . . .You can drive out of Coventry today in any direction and on the outskirts of the town you'll see vast fields solidly covered with dumped truckloads of brickbats and rubble.'

Members of the Coventry Fire Service sit down to a lunch of bread, Kraft cheese and tea. Phillip Deeming remembers other delicacies: 'there always seemed to be plenty of beetroot and Marmite, and my sandwiches always seemed to be one or the other.'

Members of Coventry Fire Brigade Band in rehearsal at Hales Street, 1941. They obviously took their music very seriously indeed.

PUBLIC SHELTERS,
GUNS & BRAKES, 1942

Dunlop's Aero Brake section. Machines were worked practically twenty-four hours a day to supply Britain's Royal Air Force with its landing gear.

George VI on his third and last wartime visit to ruined Coventry; this time with the Queen on 25 February 1942. Talking to him is the Bishop Dr Mervyn Haigh, and with the Queen is the Revd R.T. Howard. Behind (centre) walks the mayor, Alderman Moseley. On this visit the King was shown plans to rebuild the city.

The no. 20 to Bedworth picking up fares in Broadgate, shortly after its addition to the city's fleet in February 1942. In the background the Bank Chambers can be seen curving down Hertford Street. On the left is the partially burnt out Barclays Bank.

CITY OF COVENTRY

PUBLIC SHELTER ACCOMMODATION AVAILABLE IN SHOPPING AREAS

Shopping Centre. Central Area.	Nearest Shelter.	Type.	Day Accom.
1. Trinity Street	Trinity House.	Basement	458
2. Hales Street	Neales, New Buildings.	do	450
3. The Burges	Smarts, 13, The Burges	do	270
4. Bishop Street	St. Nicholas St.	Trench	280
5. Corporation St.	G.&E. Showrooms	Basement	390
	Corporation St.	Trench	430
6. Smithford St.	H. & H. Garages, West Orchard	Basement	70
7. Fleet Street and	Salvation Army Hut, Spon St.	Trench	70
8. Queen Vict. Rd.	Spon Street		
9. Spon Street	Rudge Works	Basement	924
10. Spon End	Hearsall Lane Cor.	Surface	150
	Butts, nr. Tech. College.	Trench	258
11. Warwick Row	Greyfriars Green	Trench	423
12. Hertford St.	Barracks Basement	Basement	170
13. Market Place	Old Meteor Works	do	730
14. High Street	3-6 Hay Lane	do	180
15. Jordan Well	Midland Brewery, Much Park St.	do	576
16. Much Park St.	Drapers Hall.	do	300
	Museum Site, St. Mary's Street.	do	523
17. Whitefriars St.	Brandish's Cycle Shop.	do	84
18. London Road	London Rd. In. Whitefriars St.	Trench	200
		do	130
19. Gosford Street	Cox St. cr. Grove St.	do	200
	Gosford St. Court 13	do	200
	Vequeray St. Sch.	Surface	150
20. Far Gosford St.	Gosford Green.	Trench	612
	1, Walsgrave Rd.	Basement	63
21. Ford Street	Pool Meadow Car Park	Surface	150
	Wheatley St. Sch.	do	100
	rear of Priory St. Baths	do	200
22. White Street	Bird Street	Trench	642
	Swanswell (Tennis Cts.)	do	306
23. Primrose Hill St.	15, 16, 17, Victoria Street	Basement	100
24. Victoria St.			
25. King William St.			
26. Stoney Stan. Rd.	Swanswell Rec. Ground	Surface	150
	Coventry & War. Hospital (entrance from Russell St.)	do	150
OTHER AREAS.			
27. Cheylesmore	nr. Quinton Pool	Trench	612
28. Green Lane	Stivichall Com. (Coat of Arms Bridge Rd.)	do	642
29. Earlsdon St.	Earlsdon Sch.	Surface	80
30. Albany Rd.	67, Earlsdon Ave.	Basement	70
31. Sheriff Ave.	Fletchhamstead Farm	Trench	75
32. Tile Hill Lane	Corner of By-Pass Road.	do	612
33. Moseley Ave.	Rialto Cinema	Surface	667
34. Barkers Butts Lane	Moseley Ave. (nr. School)	Trench	918
35. Radford Rd.	Radford Rec. Gd.	do	918
	Radford Sch.	do	500
	Radford Com.	do	918
36. Jubilee Cres.	Jubilee Cres.	do	306
37. Lockhurst Lane	Lockhurst Lane Railway Bridge	Under Arches	900
38. Foleshill Rd.	OBriens	Basement	588
	Courtaulds	Surface	400
	Edgwick Rec. Ground	Trench	771
39. Stoney Stan. Rd.	Nr. Websters Brickworks	do	612
40. Bell Green	opp. "Golden Fleece"	do	306
41. Walsgrave Rd.	Nr. Stoke Ch.	do	918
42. Binley Rd.	Nr. Bull's Head P.H.	Surface	100

CUT THIS OUT AND KEEP IT WITH YOU ALWAYS—
YOU MAY NEED IT AT A MINUTE'S NOTICE.

E. H. FORD, O.B.E., M.Inst.C.E., M.T.P.I.
City Engineer.

Coventry, 3rd April, 1942.

A list of public shelters near to shopping areas, published on 3 April 1942. These do not include the hundreds of street shelters scattered around the city. Surface shelters are above ground and trench shelters below. One Air Raid Warden reported that on 14 November O'Brien's shelter on the Foleshill Road took a direct hit from a UXB. The occupants, all 1,500 of them, had to be squeezed into an area big enough for 300. There they stood for eleven hours as the shelter flooded and a boiler and the bomb threatened to explode.

Looking across Broadgate and beyond to the barrage balloons, 1942. All the rubble is now gone, filling the gullys of the Warwickshire countryside. Few vehicles pass through Broadgate as petrol rationing bites harder. Philip Deeming of Allesley recalls: 'Petrol was rationed and the necessary coupons could only be obtained for essential journeys. . . . One had to keep strictly to the approved route when travelling.

A colleague who lived at Brandon had to use the Binley Road as part of his route. He occasionally visited the Forum Cinema [now a bowling alley] but had to leave his car parked in the Binley Road and walk to the cinema. Just a detour from that small journey could have caused him serious trouble.' Soon civilian use of petrol practically ended, for in March 1942 civilian petrol rationing came to an end.

War production at Dunlop Aviation in Holbrook Lane, with mainly women workers in the Gun Gear Assembly section. Dunlop developed the pneumatic gun-firing system for the Gladiator, Spitfire, Hurricane, Beaufighter and Mosquito. In a 1940 advert it was claimed that 'every enemy plane destroyed by a British fighter is shot down with the help of Dunlop gun firing gear'.

The Combination Lathe section of Dunlop, which produced wheels and pneumatic brakes, specially developed by Dunlop for fighters and fighter bombers. Next to the roof support (right) are two coal buckets, not for coal but for sand – for extinguishing incendiary bombs.

Dunlop's general war-transport fleet parked next to the water tower and newly erected hangars.

Dunlop, like many other wartime factories, had its own fire and ambulance brigades. Here we have the crews with their Climax mobile pump. Luckily the factory, some of which was camouflaged, suffered only limited damage during the war. The chief fire officer wrote in 1940: 'The co-operation of factories . . . was splendid. Most . . . were directly affected with fires, but when this happened and often after they had dealt with their own they turned out to many parts of the city. . . .'

An armed spotters' tower at Dunlop's Rim and Wheel section. At the base of the tower can be seen the badge of the Royal Warwickshire Regiment. The Dunlop site has a long history of war production, for during the First World War it was the site of White and Poppes, a munitions factory. Part of this factory can be seen next to the tower, namely the steel-framed arched windows. The factory with its workers' cottages, known as Munition Cottages, was used for the production of bullets and cannon shells. The girls who filled these shells were known locally as 'Canary Girls' as the cordite stained their hands yellow. By the factory were many underground bunkers for storing the shells. Into the site ran munitions trains which were loaded on a sunken track (at the Beake Avenue end). The site was guarded, as it was during the Second World War, the main guardhouse being in the general direction of the present Guardhouse Road.

Coventry Fire Brigade's football team lined up at the Butts Stadium, 1942. The social life of the service was most important, as it is today. The 1942 team was very successful locally.

National Fire Service crew at the rear of their base at Daventry Buildings, Cheylesmore. Opposite the station and near Quinton Pool was a trench shelter capable of holding 612 people.

605 Squad at their headquarters at the London Laundry, relaxing as they test a hose on Stoney Stanton Road.

A fireman poses by his pump, possibly in the Holbrooks area. Note the basket on the pump which acted as a filter when the pump hose was used in natural water supplies.

NSF 605 relaxing at their base on Stoney Stanton Road. Around the room were three-tiered bunks. One of the crew, Bill Boucher, recalled an incident many years ago concerning another 605 member, Ernie. 'What a character he was. Once he forgot where he was and stepped out of bed. It was a three-tier bunk; he had been at the top. I like to think of him playing his jet on a burning house, the walls of which were ready to fall on him at any moment, bombs whining all around, and his pipe in his mouth at a jaunty angle.'

The Home Guard unit from Daimler's Aero Shadow Factory in Browns Lane, 1942–3. The Guards' football team poses with other members. With the ball is Jimmy O'Sullivan, who at the time was based in Number One Block, Brooklands Hostel in Coundon. He, like many other wartime newcomers, made Coventry his home.

A small row of fairly new desirable residences, flattened either by high explosive or landmine, by the Radford Road. The area was hit by a number of mines; one remained hanging by its parachute on telephone lines outside Radford Vicarage.

Men repairing bomb damage to the Chapel of St James and St Christopher. Despite this work the council decided in the 1960s to turn the ancient wayfarers' chapel into a 'picturesque ruin.'

A battalion dinner taking place in the canteen of the Humber Works. Such events were held to boost the morale of the men and to give a feeling of being part of the team. Note on the walls the flags of Norway, France and the Free French with the Cross of Lorraine. The American flag tells us that this must be after 1941 when the Americans joined the war. Notice also the 'All Clear' sign which alternately shows an 'Alert'.

HMS *Coventry* was built by Swan, Hunter and Wigham Richardson Ltd and launched on 6 July 1917. She fought in th latter years of the First World War, survived and was converted to anti-aircraft use. HMS *Coventry* served the nation we until she was sunk at Tobruk on 14 September 1942 by German and Italian aircraft. There had been a HMS *Coventi* since the seventeenth century.

'BATTLESHIP GREY', 1943

Devastated houses in Longfellow Road, Stoke. In the foreground stand the remains of a brick surface shelter, built for passers-by and nearby householders. Philip Deeming recalls: 'I can still remember my mother going into the shelter . . . taking her knitting bag . . . insurance policies . . . and the budgerigar . . . at one time she was holding the wall of the shelter . . . hoping to prevent it being blown on top of us.'

Holy Trinity Church in 1943, bearing the message erected by the Revd W.G. Clitheroe; this read 'It all depends on me, and I depend on God.' This reflected Clitheroe's belief that he 'was never prepared to face the possibility of losing Trinity whilst I could fight to save it'. Clitheroe added: 'it is the standpoint of the warrior mind. . . . Not the individual alone, not God alone . . . but trusting in God to give strength.' The warrior in Clitheroe was reflected in the fact that he wanted a gun on the roof of Trinity, so 'we could be offensive as well as defensive.'

Part of a group of twenty-five wartime buses being repainted battleship grey. The bus in the foreground, no. 309, was part of a group of four new buses delivered to the Corporation in January 1943. These buses, produced up to the spring of 1943, all had upholstered seats. Those made after May were 'austerity' buses, with basic wooden slatted seats.

The same buses from a different angle. No. 287 was delivered to the city in September 1942 bearing the livery of Coventry; maroon and cream.

A grey Bedworth bus, no. 303, passes through Broadgate, 1943. This Guy Arab bus with Manchester Corporation-style bodywork was one of many buses added to the fleet in early 1943 owing to a shortage of vehicles. This was not only because of bomb damage to the fleet but also because Coventry had an ever-expanding population, due to war production. Lack of fuel also meant restricted travel and no buses after 4 p.m.

Buses passing through the east side of Broadgate early in 1943. In between the buses can be seen Lyon's Café, a favourite from pre-war days. The upper section of the building was destroyed and the ground floor adapted and used until 1947, when the east side had a block of temporary shops built.

Mr Joseph Ivens (centre rear) with his fire-watch party at the rear of Allesly Old Road. Mr Ivens joined the Coventry Volunteer Fire Brigade in 1921 and served until 1934. Little did he know that within a few short years he would be setting up one of the city's many local fire-watch crews.

Demolition of Owen Owen photographed from Cross Cheaping. Despite the fact that the building was burnt out it looks strangely untarnished.

The Owen Owen building had been newly opened only seven years earlier. This picture, taken in August or September 1943, looks up Trinity Street into Broadgate and beyond. The grey bus and standard livery buses ply for fares on the left.

The 500th De Havilland Merlin-engined Mosquito FB VI stands outside the Standards factory at Canley. This fast fighter-bomber, a stalwart of the RAF, was first produced by Standard in June 1943. Production ceased in December 1945 with the completion of the 1,066th Standard Mosquito. In front of the plane from the left stand Jim Thompson, Cecil Olorenshaw, Reg Addison, Charlie Newin, Bill Wanley, Bill Guessey and Frank Perkins.

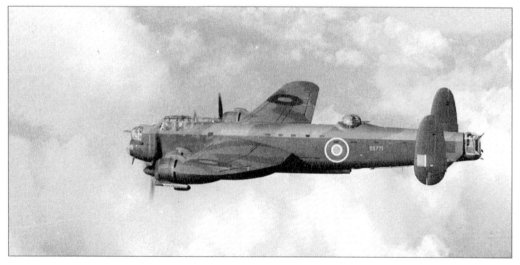

A Coventry-built AWA Lancaster bomber. The first model of this well-remembered bomber, the Lancaster I was completed in August 1942. When production of Whitleys ceased in 1943 work centred around the development of the Hercules-engined Lancaster IIs and IIIs.

VISIONS OF THE FUTURE, 1944

Humber crew during their three-man drill in a late wartime competition when the raids had ceased.

Morris Motors fire crew from Mile Lane taking part in a drill competition at Courthouse Green. The Chief Fire Officer in 1940 wrote: 'the factories and premises which were not so seriously damaged by fire were mostly firms which had trained fire brigades.'

The same crew connecting up their Coventry Climax fire pump, bearing its wartime '24.G' Coventry area code.

Members of the Dane Road (Stoke Park School) fire station during a recreation period. During the latter years of the war, when there was little threat to the 'Home Front', many men in essential services such as the fire service were called up by the forces, leaving the women to carry on the good work.

Ladies of the Dane Road crew, including Mrs Tallis and Josephine Player, clearing an area for 'recreational sunbathing'. This much amused the remaining men in the station until they were ordered to assist the ladies in the task.

In 1938 the newly elected City Council decided that Coventry needed an architectural department, a rarity in day when such work was usually under the auspices of the City Engineer. Out of sixty-nine applicants for the new City Architect, 29-year-old Donald Gibson was chosen. The new department, manned mainly by young men, began work in January 1939. Even in those early days before the city centre's destruction Gibson and his team began putting together ideas that would lead to large rebuilding schemes and demolition of the old centre. Gibson was not the first, for before him the city planning officer, Ernest Ford, put forward his idea for a new road system and traffic free shopping. The planners' dream of rebuilding Coventry unexpectedly became a reality after the night of 14 November. Within a month of that fateful night meetings were being held to discuss rebuilding. In February 1941 Donald Gibson and Ernest Ford put forward separate ideas for rebuilding; Gibson's was accepted as the blue-print for the future. Above can be seen Gibson's vision for the first pedestrian precinct. Initially delivery vehicles only were to have access to the rear of the buildings, but by 1945 local traders had forced Gibson to revise his plan and turn Market Way into a road, as they believed people would not walk from car-parks. George Hodgkinson, ex-Mayor and leader of the Redevelopment Committee, supported Gibson's plans and suggested that a water feature should run down the length of the precinct (a in the picture). These plans too were stopped when a major store objected. The plans, however, were not final and would be revised in the future.

In February 1939 the council mooted the idea of a new civic centre. Gibson and his team put on an exhibition promoting the vista envisaged in the above drawing. It consisted of a civic centre, gallery, library, civic offices and a college. On the left was planned a civic park down to Pool Meadow, once again a pool. On the right Trinity Street runs through an arch into Hertford Street.

A wartime (c. 1944) view of the future, including Broadgate Island and Godiva. This plan included demolition of the cathedral walls, Georgian Priory Row, County Hall and the medieval buildings above St Mary's Hall.

Donald Gibson's vision of Broadgate published early in 1945, before war's end, in a booklet called *Coventry's Future*. Note the two elephants on pillars at the entrance to the precinct, also the Godiva statue (already designed) on Broadgate island, which became a reality in 1949. The arch into Hertford Street became a simple drive-under bridge.

During the latter years of the war Donald Gibson worked on various designs for experimental pre-fabricated buildings, as a quick way of rehousing Coventry's homeless. One such building was the 'Coventry Experimental House', which had its steel-frame body and roof erected in one day. Here we see the second stage, the fixing of cast blocks to the main structure – and not a blob of mortar in sight.

S E C T I O N E I G H T

WAR'S END, 1945

This photograph actually dates from about 1946, and shows EWK 240, the Cross Cheaping bus, which had been miraculously restored to service back in 1942. Coventry Transport engineering staff took great pride in the rebuilding of EWK 240, their way of saying 'Up yours, Mr Hitler.'

Broadgate at war's end; normality is returning to the city. The citizens await the great rebuilding. The post office below the bank in Hertford Street had four floors; it now has three, probably because of fire damage in November 1940.

Looking down on AWA's main Baginton plant, 1945. This factory was opened in 1936 and its huge hangars were used for the final construction stages of Whitleys, Albermarles, Manchesters, Lancasters, Wellingtons and Lincolns. Note the Lincoln bombers outside the hangars. Baginton airport (bottom right) was for a short time the base for Spitfire and Hurricane crews, later used for air reconnaissance.

A Lincoln Mark II at Baginton, March 1945. Lincolns were built here between 1945 and 1948. They were also brought to Baginton for maintenance and conversion for use in the Far East. Note the now rare Whitley Bomber in the background.

This amazing aeroplane is the AW52 Flying Wing, built by Armstrong Whitworth at its Baginton Works. It first flew on 13 November 1947, but was conceived before the end of the war. As a result of wartime tests in early 1946 an engineless glider version was flown, towed 15,000 ft above Baginton by a Lancaster bomber. Each test flight ended with a forced landing, but valuable lessons were learned by such tests. The second version of the wing was powered by two Rolls-Royce Nene engines, which were remarkably quiet as they were set deep within the wing. It was covered with a new material called 'Alclad', a metal skin (which would come back into use with the Concord and Vulcan), and had a wing span of nearly 100 ft. The plane could travel at well over 350 m.p.h. and during one test flight it developed a flapping motion and went into a dive. The test pilot 'Jo' Lancaster had to leave the plane, and became the first man in history to use an ejector seat. Jo landed with fractures and bruises, like the plane – which crashed and was practically undamaged. The problems, however, were soon corrected on the second prototype and the flying wing looked set to have a bright future, until the Government withdrew funding and the project was forced to end. The flying wing concept is now considered by designers to be the future of the aeroplane. Such craft could not have existed if not for Sir Frank Whittle, who was born in Newcombe Road, Earlsdon, in 1907. Sir Frank conceived the idea of the jet engine in 1928, ran successful tests in 1937 and the first test flight in 1941. But for the lack of Government interest, Whittle later stated that we could have had a jet-powered RAF by 1942.

After almost six years of war Germany surrendered, and 8 May 1945 was declared VE (Victory in Europe) Day. Coventry, like the rest of the country, celebrated; thousands gathered in Broadgate to hear Churchill's victory speech relayed by radio. The Hippodrome Orchestra played on the Hippodrome steps – and amongst the revelry a small group of American solders are remembered for causing concern as they threw fireworks into the crowd. Those who were not in the city centre were celebrating at the hundreds of street parties which took place around the city. The fare at these parties consisted mainly of jam tarts, cakes, puddings, bread and butter and of course the sacred liquid which saw Britain through the blitz, namely tea. George Jeary of Longford recalls the day: 'When VE Day arrived my father, who was in business at Brookville Stores (Holbrook Lane), along with my mother was asked by the owner of the Lyric cinema for the biggest Union Jack he could get. My dad went to Birmingham and came back with a car load, with one out-size one for the Lyric. They sold like hot cakes and people were queueing for them. VE Day saw me and the entire Youth Fellowship of Lockhurst Lane Methodist Church enjoying a dance around a bonfire at the rear of the Brookville, a bombed cinema. Being the owner of amplifying equipment I was in demand at several street parties. . . . The Sunningdale Avenue party had Christmas tree lights out in the trees . . . everyone sat down to a great feed with party hats. . . . Weeks before the wives . . . had stored food, made jellies etc. At dusk a film show was put on for the children, followed by a dance for the grown ups. The local bobby joined in as well. Similar proceedings happened at Olive Street. . . . At Freeman Street I took along a home made arc lamp . . . I didn't know sufficient about electricity to realise I was operating a highly dangerous contraption. I was on a bay window ... and it started to rain. Needless to say the lamp was disconnected and the party continued in a light drizzle. In those days everyone helped everyone else.' The photograph was taken in Stevenson Road, Keresley.

The Revd R.T. Howard leads a service of celebration and prayer in the damp ruins of St Michael's on VE Day, 8 May 1945. It is said that after his cathedral was destroyed Howard's pulpit was the rubble. The people of Coventry had lost many in combat and 1,236 at home. The city endured 41 air raids, between 18 August 1940 and 3 August 1942. There were also 373 siren alerts.

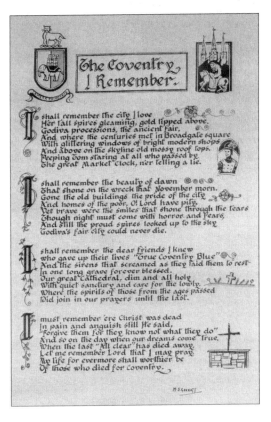

The Coventry I Remember was written by the late Miriam Garrett. Proceeds of its sale went to the people of Stalingrad, who suffered greatly when besieged by the Germans.

The grey clouds of war are replaced by bright skies as the people of Stevenson Road, Keresley, celebrate the end of war in Europe. Troops were still fighting, but VJ (Victory in Japan) Day was only months away and the world would once again be at peace. The waste ground behind once contained bombed houses; above the celebration bonfire hangs an effigy of Hitler. Soon the men would start returning home. Mary Dalton, now living in Kenilworth recalls, '. . . many children born during their absence wondered who was the strange man in Mummy's bed!' Mary's husband eventually got to hug his son for the first time when he was four years old, 'amid tears of joy' – happiness reigned supreme as peace came back to the land.

ACKNOWLEDGEMENTS

Many thanks to the following, without whom it would have been impossible to compile this book: Midland Air Museum (Barry James); Dunlop Aviation (Diane Plunkett); Museum of British Road Transport (Steve Bagley and Barry Collins); Phil Consadine; John Ashby; Roger Bailey; Cliff Barlow; John Stanton; Martyn Hammond; Les Fannon; James Armer; Gil Rowbottom; Jim O'Sullivan; Ina Harrison; and Coventry City Archives (Roger Vaughan), The photos copyright City Archives are pages (top and bottom): 78, 79, 100, 132; (top): 80, 101; (bottom): 87, 93, 135.

Many thanks to the following who offered information and other valuable assistance: Heather Head; J.&J. Cash's Ltd (Ruth Shannon); Local Studies, Central Library (Andrew Mealey); West Midlands Fire Service (K. Clarkson); Peugeot; Coventry & Warwickshire Hospital; Keresley Women's Institute (Barbara Thomas); George Jeary; Michael Newman; George Fearn; Mary Dalton; John Bevan; Philip Deeming; Winifred McCartney; Martyn Hammond; Tim Padfield (Crown Copyright Officer); and Dave Morgan.

Visit our website and discover thousands of other History Press books.

www.thehistorypress.co.uk